Container Gardening

STEP-BY-STEP
Container Gardening

Stephanie Donaldson

Photographs by John Freeman

SMITHMARK

© Anness Publishing Limited 1995

This edition published in 1995 by
SMITHMARK Publishers Inc.
16 East 32nd Street
New York
NY 10016

SMITHMARK books are available for bulk purchase for sales
promotion and for premium use. For details write or call
the manager of special sales, SMITHMARK Publishers Inc.
16 East 32nd Street, New York, 10016; (212) 532–6600

ISBN 0 8317 6548 8

Produced by Anness Publishing Limited
1 Boundary Row
London SE1 8HP

Editorial Director: Joanna Lorenz
Series Editor: Lindsay Porter
Designer: Peter Laws
Jacket Designer: Peter Butler
Photographer: John Freeman
Stylist: Stephanie Donaldson

Printed and bound in Hong Kong

CONTENTS

INTRODUCTION

You don't need expert knowledge to be a successful gardener, and if you own a houseplant or a pot of parsley, you are already container gardening. Today, good quality container-grown plants are available all through the year, and skills such as seed sowing, potting-on and taking cuttings, although interesting, are no longer essential. There is nothing wrong with this form of "instant" gardening. By buying plants that are nearing maturity, you are saved the time-consuming and uncertain business of rearing the plants, and you can try out different shape and color combinations before you buy the plants by simply grouping them together.

Gardening in containers has other advantages: like furniture, containers can be moved around to create a new look, with pride of place given to those plants that are performing best. Unlike plants in the border, the containers can simply be moved into the background once flowering is over.

The plants are only a part of the equation, and you can be creative with your choice of containers. Shops and garden centers stock an ever-increasing range of containers to suit every budget, from magnificent Italian olive jars to humble plastic pots. Junk shops and garage sales are also a rich source of objects that can take on a new lease of life as a planter — a blackened cooking pot with a hole in its base is useless for its original purpose, but is ideal as a container of character and can be bought for pennies.

Whether you are a complete novice or an experienced gardener, container gardening is an accessible, enjoyable and colorful way to brighten your surroundings.

Seed Sowing

Some plants are very easy to sow from seed – sunflowers rarely disappoint, even if you are a complete beginner.

1 Fill the pot with seed soil mix. Gently firm and level the surface by pressing down on the soil mix using a pot of the same size.

2 When sowing large seeds, such as sunflowers, use a dibber, cane or pencil to make holes for each seed. Plant the seeds and then firmly tap the side of the pot with the flat of your hand to fill the holes with soil mix. Water from above using a fine rose on a watering can, or by standing the pot in a saucer of water until the surface of the soil mix is moist. Cover the pot with a black plastic bag as most seeds germinate best in a warm dark place. Check daily and bring into the light when the seedlings are showing.

3 When sowing small seeds they should be thinly scattered on the surface of the soil mix and then covered with just enough sieved soil mix to conceal them. Firm the surface using another pot and then treat in the same way as large seeds.

Potting-on

Sooner or later plants need repotting. Young seedlings, shown here, don't thrive in large pots. Divide the plants, if necessary, and plant them in pots the same size as the one they were previously grown in.

1 Seedlings will probably be ready to move into larger pots when the roots start to emerge through the holes in the base of the pot. To check, gently remove the rootball from the pot and if there are plenty of roots showing, you will know the plants are ready for a move.

2 If there is more than one seedling in the pot, gently break each seedling away with a good rootball. (Some plants hate to have their roots disturbed. The information on the seed packet will tell you this. These seeds are best sown individually in peat pots.)

3 Lower the rootball of the plant into the pot and gently pour soil mix around it, lightly pressing the soil mix around the roots and stem. It doesn't matter if the stem of the seedling is buried deeper than it was previously as long as the leaves are well clear of the soil. Water using a can with a fine rose.

Watering

Too much water is as bad as too little – get the balance right and let your plants thrive.

1 The best way to avoid overwatering a plant is to stand the pot in a saucer and water into the saucer. The plant's roots can then take up moisture as needed.

2 Most plants are quite happy to be watered from above, as here. This is not recommended for plants with velvety leaves such as African violets. They should be watered in the saucer.

3 Houseplants enjoy being sprayed with water, but in hard water areas you should use rain water or bottled water.

Saucers and Feet

Saucers are available for plastic and clay pots. They act as water reservoirs for the plants, and are used under houseplants to protect the surface they are standing on. Clay saucers must be fully glazed if they are used indoors or they will leave marks. Clay feet are available for terracotta pots. They will prevent the pot becoming waterlogged, but this also means that in a sunny position the pot will dry out very quickly and may need extra watering.

1 Plastic saucers can be used to line containers which are not waterproof, such as this wooden apple basket.

Planting in Terracotta Pots

Terracotta pots are always popular, but need some preparation before planting.

1 With terracotta pots it is essential to provide some form of drainage material in the base of the container. With small pots this can be broken pieces of pot, known as crocks, or gravel.

2 Cover the drainage material with a layer of soil mix before planting in the container.

3 When planting in large pots, recycle styrofoam plant trays as drainage material. Lumps of styrofoam are excellent for this purpose and as they retain warmth they are of additional benefit to the plant.

Planting in Plastic Pots

When buying plastic pots check that the drainage holes are open. Some manufacturers mark the holes, but leave it to the customer to punch them out or drill them as required.

1 With plastic pots there is no need to use any drainage material at the base of the container, simply cover the bottom of the pot with a layer of soil mix.

Plant Supports

Climbing plants need support even in containers. Support can be provided by using stakes which can be pushed into the pot, or a trellis which is fastened to a wall or a free standing frame.

Hanging Baskets

The key to successful hanging baskets is in the preparation. Time taken in preparing the basket for planting will be rewarded with a long-lasting colorful display. Slow-release plant food granules incorporated into the soil mix when planting will ensure that the plants receive adequate nutrients throughout the growing season. It is essential to water hanging baskets every day, even in overcast weather, as they dry out very quickly. There are various ways to line a hanging basket.

1 When buying a hanging basket, make sure that the chains are detachable. By unhooking one of the chains, they can be placed to one side of the basket, allowing you to work freely.

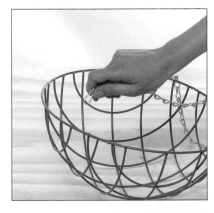

2 Traditionally, hanging baskets are lined with sphagnum moss. This looks very attractive and plants can be introduced at any point in the side of the basket. As sphagnum moss does tend to dry out rather faster than other liners, it is advisable to use a soil mix containing water-retaining gel.

3 Coir fiber liners are a practical substitute for moss. Although not as good to look at, the coir will soon be hidden as the plants grow. The slits allow for planting in the side of the basket.

4 Cardboard liners are clean and easy to use. They are made in various sizes to fit most hanging baskets.

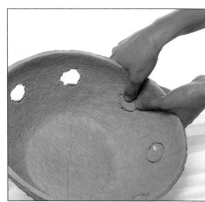

5 Press out the marked circles on the cardboard liner if you wish to plant into the side of it.

Common Pests

Vine weevils *(above)*
These white grubs are a real problem. The first sign of an infestation is the sudden collapse of the plant, which has died as a result of the weevil eating its roots. Systemic insecticides or natural predators can be used as a preventative, but once a plant has been attacked it is usually too late. Never re-use the soil from an affected plant.

Caterpillars *(above)*
The occasional caterpillar can be simply picked off the plant and disposed of as you see fit, but a major infestation can strip a plant before your eyes. Contact insecticides are usually very effective in these cases.

Slugs and snails
As a preventative measure, smear a circle of petroleum jelly below the rim of the pot as the slugs and snails will not cross this. If there is already a problem with slugs in the pot, slug pellets should deal with any resident pests.

Scale insects
These can be very troublesome on container-grown plants, particularly on those with waxy leaves, such as bay, citrus, *Ficus* and

Stephanotis. The first sign is often a sticky substance on the leaves. If you look under the leaves and at the leaf joints you may be able to spot the scales. A serious infestation will be indicated by a black sooty mold. The scale insect's waxy coating makes it resistant to contact insecticides, so use of a systemic insecticide is essential. As scale insects develop over quite a long period it is important to treat regularly for a couple of months.

Whitefly *(above)*
As their name indicates, these are tiny white flies which flutter in clouds when disturbed from their feeding places on the undersides of leaves. Whitefly are particularly troublesome in conservatories where a dry atmosphere will encourage them to breed. Keep the air as moist as possible. Contact insecticides will need more than one application to deal with an infestation, but a systemic insecticide will protect the plant for weeks.

Insecticides

There are two main types of insecticide available to combat common pests.

Contact insecticides
These must be sprayed directly onto the insects to be effective. Most organic insecticides work this way, but they generally kill all insects, even beneficial ones such as dragon flies and ladybugs. Try to remove these before spraying the infected plant.

Mealy bugs
These look like spots of white mold. Like scale insects they are hard to shift and regular treatment with a systemic insecticide is the best solution.

Aphids
One of the most common plant pests. These green sap-sucking insects feed on the tender growing tips of plants. Most insecticides are effective against aphids. Choose one that will not harm ladybugs as aphids are a favorite food of theirs.

Red Spider mite *(above)*
This is another insect that thrives indoors in dry conditions. Constant humidity will reduce the chance of an infestation. The spider mite is barely visible to the human eye, but infestation is indicated by the presence of fine webs and mottling of the plant's leaves. To treat an infestation, it is best to move the plant outdoors if the weather is suitable, spray with an insecticide and allow the plant time to recover before bringing it back indoors.

Systemic insecticides
These work by being absorbed by the plant's root or leaf system and killing the insects that come into contact with the plant. This will work for difficult pests such as vine weevils which are hidden in the soil, and scale insects, which protect themselves from above with a scaly cover.

BIOLOGICAL CONTROL

Commercial growers now use biological control in their greenhouses, which means natural predators are introduced to eat the pest population. Although not all are suitable for the amateur gardener, they can be used in conservatories for dealing with pests such as whitefly.

Feeding your Plants

It is not generally known that most potting soil mixes contain only sufficient food for six weeks of plant growth. After that the plants will slowly starve unless other food is introduced. There are several products available, all of which are easy to use.

Slow-release plant food granules
These will keep your container plants in prime condition and are very easy to use. One application lasts six months, whereas most other plant foods need to be applied at two-week intervals.

Composted stable manure
This is a good organic plant food and will also improve the condition of the soil. Greedy plants like tomatoes and fruit trees love a good mulch of manure which will provide them with extra food and conserve moisture.

Liquid feeds
These are available in many formulations. Generally the organic liquid manures and seaweed feeds are brown in color and should be mixed to look like very weak tea. The chemical feeds are frequently colored to prevent them being mistaken for soft drinks. The best way to avoid accidents with garden chemicals is to mix up only as much as you need on each occasion and never store them in soft drink bottles. Liquid feeds should be applied every other week in the growing season. Don't be tempted to mix a feed stronger than is recommended – it can burn the roots of the plant and it certainly won't make it grow any faster.

Soil Mixes

Soil mixes come in various formulations suitable for different plant requirements. A standard potting soil mix is usually peat-based and is suitable for all purposes. Different soil mixes can be mixed together for specific plant needs.

Standard soil mix
The majority of soil mixes available at the garden center are peat-based with added fertilizers.

Ericaceous soil mix
A peat-based soil mix, but with no added lime, essential for rhododendrons, camellias and gardenias in containers.

Container soil mix
A peat-based soil mix with moisture-retaining granules and added fertilizer, especially formulated for hanging baskets and containers.

Peat-free soil mix
Manufacturers are beginning to offer soil mixes using materials from renewable resources such as coir fiber. They are used in the same way as peat-based soil mixes.

Loam-based soil mix
This uses sterilized loam as the main ingredient, with fertilizers to supplement the nutrients in the loam. Although much heavier than peat-based soil mix, it can be lightened by mixing with peat-free soil mix. Ideal for long-term container planting.

Mulches

A mulch is a layer of protective material placed over the soil. It helps to retain moisture, conserve warmth, suppress weeds and prevents soil splash on foliage and flowers.

Composted bark
Bark is an extremely effective mulch and as it rots down it also conditions the soil. It works best when spread at least 8 cm (3 in) thick and is therefore not ideal for small containers. It is derived from renewable resources.

Stones
Smooth stones can be used as decorative mulch for large container-grown plants. You can save stones dug out of the garden or buy stones from garden centers. Cat owners will also find they keep cats from using the soil surrounding large houseplants as a litter tray.

Clay granules
Clay granules are widely used for hydroculture, but can also be used to mulch houseplants. When placing a plant in a cachepot, fill all around the pot with granules. When watered, the granules absorb moisture, which is then released slowly to create a moist microclimate for the plant.

Gravel
Gravel makes a decorative mulch for container plants and also provides the correct environment for plants such as Alpines. It is available in a variety of sizes and colors which can be matched to the scale and colors of the plants used.

Water-retaining gel

One of the main problems for most container gardeners is the amount of watering required to keep the plants thriving. Adding water-retaining gels to soil mixes will certainly help reduce this task. Sachets of gel are available from garden centers.

1 Pour the recommended amount of water into a bowl.

2 Scatter the gel over the surface, stirring occasionally until it has absorbed the water.

3 Add to your soil mix at the recommended rate.

4 Mix the gel in thoroughly before using it for planting.

Underwatering

A thirsty plant will withdraw water from its leaves leaving them limp, while retaining as much moisture as possible in its roots and stems. Many plants can be revived before it is too late.

I This plant will revive when it has sufficient water. Peat soil mix will not easily absorb water once it has dried right out. Plunge the pot into a bucket of water and leave it to soak for at least an hour to ensure a full recovery. Standing a pot in a saucer helps conserve moisture.

2 By the next day the plant should have retained its former vigor. Always make sure the soil mix is dry before plunging the pot in water, as an overwatered plant will also wilt.

3 This plant is beyond help. Its leaves have gone from limp to brittle and its chances of a recovery are very remote indeed. Soaking the pot in water may help.

Overwatering

While most plants thrive in humid conditions over-watering will kill them as certainly as underwatering.

I The soil mix in this pot is very wet, as indicated by the brown leaves on this geranium. Some healthy leaves remain on the plant, but they too will turn brown and die unless it is allowed to dry out.

2 The plant on the left has been overwatered and is beginning to look sickly. The plant on the right has received the correct amount of water.

3 This cactus has been thoroughly overwatered and will not recover. A desert is a dry place and this plant requires similar conditions in your home.

The Furnished Garden

Container-gardening offers a flexibility impossible with traditional beds and borders. The containers can be repositioned when the plants are past their best, to allow specimens at their peak to move to center stage. Containers can also be used to embellish a forgotten corner or hide unattractive features. Think of your containers as garden furniture and use them to hide unsightly objects.

1 This terrace of old brick and stone is attractive in its own right, but is not as colorful as it might be.

1 This shady area next to a driveway has been gravelled to break up the effect of a large area of paving but still looks bleak and uninteresting.

2 The addition of a variety of containers with flowering plants completes the picture and adds color and depth to the scene.

2 The addition of shade-loving plants in containers has transformed this corner. Even though some wires and a downpipe may still be visible, there is so much else to interest the eye that they are easily overlooked.

PLANT COMBINATIONS

The basket on the left uses the differing leaf shapes and colors of the plants to make an exciting foliage display. Look out for good plant associations in garden centers, parks, and other people's gardens and try them at home. Don't be afraid to experiment, it's what gardening is all about.

Types of Container

Part of the fun of container gardening is experimenting with the different planters available. Garden centers stock an increasing variety of styles, and junk shops, garage sales and flea markets are also worth a visit.

Novelty containers
Old gardening or cooking implements which are no longer suitable for their original purpose can be spray-painted or stencilled.

Terracotta pots
Almost every style and size imaginable is available in terracotta, from huge floor-standing planters for trees, to simple rustic flower pots and wall planters.

Painted clay pots
These will add an additional spot of color in the house or garden. Buy ready-painted or paint your own in soft pastels or bright Mediterranean colors.

Baskets
These add a wonderful country feel to any display, and look delightful planted with spring bulbs. Always line before planting, or use simply as a cachepot.

Wire baskets
Lined with sphagnum moss, these make pretty containers for spring bulbs or other small flowering plants.

Galvanized tinware
These are available both new and secondhand in all shapes and sizes, from small buckets to tin baths; wall planters to freestanding pots.

Window boxes
These are available in a range of different materials, from terracotta to bark. This planter has a verdigris effect, but is in fact made of lightweight fiberglass.

Spring Hanging Basket

Once the spring flowers have started to brighten our gardens, walls can look rather bare. This hanging basket can be planted in the early spring as it will survive frosts. It will add a welcome splash of color and provide some fresh parsley for the kitchen.

MATERIALS AND TOOLS
Hanging basket, 30 cm (12 in)
 diameter
Sphagnum moss
Hanging basket soil mix
Plastic pot (optional)
Slow-release plant food granules
Trowel

PLANTS
2 strips of young parsley plants
3 small-flowered yellow violets
3 ivies

ivy

parsley

violet

1 Unclip the chain from one of the fixing points. This will prevent it from becoming tangled up with the plants while you are planting the basket.

2 Line the base and the bottom half of the basket with a generous layer of moss.

3 Fill the moss-lined area with hanging basket soil mix, leaving about 3 cm (1 in) of moss exposed.

4 Plant half of the parsley plants into the side of the basket. You can do this by either feeding the rootball inwards through the wire or the leaves outwards, which ever works best. It is easier to see what you are doing if you stand the basket on a plant pot and it will also be more stable.

5 Line the remainder of the basket with moss, tucking it around the parsley plants which you have already planted.

6 Fill the remainder of the basket with soil mix.

GARDENER'S TIP

Wire-working companies are now
making copies of old hanging baskets
like the one in this project. They
won't have the much-used look of this
one, but a few seasons planting will
soon remedy that.

   Baskets are usually hung from a
bracket securely fixed to a wall or
gate post.

Plant in early spring.

7 Plant the violets, ivies and remaining
parsley plants in the top of the basket,
scattering a tablespoon of slow-release
plant food granules onto the top of the
soil mix. Firm the plants in place and
water. Re-attach the chain to the basket
and hang it in full or partial sun.

Miniature Spring Garden

Terracotta pots filled with crocuses, irises and primroses, nestling in a bed of moss, make a delightful scaled-down spring garden which would fit on the smallest balcony or even a windowsill. Choose containers of contrasting shapes for best effect.

MATERIALS AND TOOLS
Terracotta seed tray
2 terracotta pots, 12 cm (5 in) high
Crocks
Standard soil mix
Sheet moss
Trowel

PLANTS
3 primroses
Pot of Reticulata irises in bud
Pot of crocuses in bud

crocus

Reticulata iris

sheet moss

primrose

GARDENER'S TIP

Once the irises and crocuses are past their best, hide them behind other pots to die down and dry out before starting them into growth again in the autumn.

Plant in early spring.

GARDENER'S TIP

After the primrose plants have finished flowering they will send out glossy green leaves all summer long if they are kept in a cool shady spot and are watered regularly. Next year, after flowering they can be divided up to provide you with many more plants.

1 Cover the drainage holes of the seed tray and the two pots with crocks.

2 Half-fill the seed tray with soil mix. Before planting the primroses, loosen the roots by gently squeezing the root ball and teasing the roots loose. The plants will establish themselves far better in the surrounding soil mix if you do this.

3 Arrange the primroses in the seed tray and, once you are happy with their positioning, fill in with soil mix around the plants, pressing down around the plants to ensure they are firmly planted.

4 Arrange the sheet moss around the plants so that all the soil mix is hidden.

5 Remove the irises from their plastic pot and slip them into the terracotta pot. Bed them in with a little extra soil mix if necessary and then arrange moss around the base of the stems.

6 Repeat this process with the crocuses and then water all the pots.

Wine Case Herb Garden

Add a coat of varnish to an old wine case and make an attractive and durable container for a miniature herb garden. The container can be placed near the kitchen door or on the balcony.

MATERIALS AND TOOLS
Wooden wine case
Pliers
Sandpaper
Paintbrush
Light oak semi-matt varnish
Crocks or similar drainage material
Standard soil mix with ⅓ added coarse grit
Slow-release plant food granules
Bark mulch
Trowel

PLANTS
Selection of 7 herbs, such as sage, chives, parsley, mint, tarragon, lemon thyme and creeping thyme

chives

parsley

GARDENER'S TIP

Some herbs like cool, partial shade while others like hot, dry, free-draining soil. A mixed herb garden will thrive for one growing season only.

Plant in spring.

1 Remove any wire staples from around the edges of the box and sand down any rough edges. Apply two coats of varnish on the inside and outside of the box, allowing the varnish to dry thoroughly between coats. Cover the base of the box with a layer of crocks or similar drainage material.

2 Before planting, plan how you are going to arrange the plants in the container to achieve a pleasing balance of color, height and shape.

3 Fill the box with gritty soil mix and, working from one end of the box to the other, begin planting. Loosen the rootballs before planting, as this will help the plants to root into the surrounding soil mix.

4 Add the remaining plants. Scatter 2 tablespoons of slow-release plant food granules on the surface of the soil mix. Firm in the plants and mulch with a layer of bark, to retain moisture and prevent soil splashing the foliage. Water well.

Japanese-style Planter

A wooden apple barrel makes an inexpensive container for this Japanese maple. The tree is surrounded with moss and stones to create the effect of a Japanese garden. This planted container is designed to be very lightweight and would be ideal for a roof terrace or balcony.

MATERIALS AND TOOLS
Apple barrel or similar wooden tub
Plastic saucer to fit the bottom of the
    container
Slow-release plant food granules
Bag of perlite or styrofoam packing
    material
Sheet moss
Large stones

PLANTS
Japanese maple (*Acer palmatum
    dissectum*)

Japanese maple

I Place the plastic saucer in the base of the container.

2 Stand the tree in its pot in the saucer. Scatter half a tablespoon of slow-release plant food granules on the surface of the soil mix. Fill the area around the pot with perlite or styrofoam.

3 Cover the surface of the perlite or styrofoam with sheet moss interspersed with stones. Place in full or partial sun, and water regularly.

GARDENER'S TIP
The tree should be checked annually to see if it needs repotting. If roots are showing through the base of the pot this is a sure sign that the tree should be moved into a larger pot. If weight is not a consideration use clay granules instead of perlite or styrofoam.

Plant at any time of the year.

Spring Display in a Copper Boiler

A battered old wash boiler makes an attractive and characterful container for a display of white tulips underplanted with purple violets and evergreen periwinkles.

MATERIALS AND TOOLS
Copper boiler, 60 cm (24 in) diameter
Plastic pot, 20 cm (8 in) diameter
Standard soil mix
Trowel

PLANTS
20 white tulip bulbs or tulips in bud
5 purple violets
2 periwinkles (*Vinca minor* was used here)

tulip

periwinkle

violet

1 Place an upturned 20 cm (8 in) pot in the base of the boiler before filling it with soil mix. This will save on the amount of soil mix used and will not have any effect on the growth of the plants as they will still have plenty of room to grow.

2 If you are planting tulip bulbs, half-fill the container with soil mix, arrange the bulbs evenly over the surface and then cover them with a good 15 cm (6 in) of soil mix. This should be done in late autumn.

3 Do the underplanting in the early spring. The soil mix will have settled in the container and should be topped up to within 8 cm (3 in) of the rim. Remove the violets from their pots. Gently squeeze the rootballs and loosen the roots to aid the plants' growth.

4 Plant one violet in the center and four around the edges. Scoop out the soil by hand to avoid damaging the growing tips of the tulips beneath the soil.

5 Plant a periwinkle either side of the central violet, again loosening the rootballs.

GARDENER'S TIP

Lift the tulips when they have finished flowering and hang them up to dry in a cool airy place. They can be replanted later in the winter to flower again next year. Provided you pick off the dead flowers the violets will flower all summer. For a summer display, lift the central violet and plant a standard white marguerite in the center of the container.

Plant bulbs in autumn or plants in bud in spring. Plant the violets and periwinkle in spring.

6 Alternatively, if you are planting tulips in bud, the whole scheme should be planted at the same time. Work from one side of the pot to the other, interplanting the tulips with the violets and periwinkles. Press down firmly around the tulips or they will work themselves loose in windy weather. Position in sun or partial shade.

Auricula Theatre

In the late 18th and early 19th century "Primrose Feasts" were held, where prize auricula primroses were displayed in specially built theatres. This simple interpretation of an old tradition will create an interesting focal point in your garden.

MATERIALS AND TOOLS
Pine corner shelf unit
Steel wool or sandpaper
Paintbrush
Matt black exterior paint
Wall plugs and screws
Crocks
2 terracotta pots, 10 cm (4 in) high
　(preferably old)
Loam-based soil mix with
　⅓ added grit

PLANTS
2 auricula primroses

auricula primrose

GARDENER'S TIP

An ordinary shelf unit will display the plants as effectively as a corner shelf. Use the theatre to display other dramatic plants when the auriculas are out of season: bright red geraniums, pot marigolds and nasturtiums in high summer, zinnias in late summer, and pansies during the autumn and winter.

Plant in spring.

1 Rub down the shelves with steel wool or sandpaper – this is particularly important if the wood has been treated with wax in the past.

2 Apply at least two coats of the paint to the shelves inside and out. Remember this is going to be outdoors and will need to be well sealed to protect it against the weather. Allow the paint to dry and then fasten it to the wall of your choice using wall plugs and screws.

3 Place a crock in the bottom of each terracotta pot. Gently remove each auricula from its plastic pot, supporting the plant as shown in the picture as the soil mix is likely to be quite crumbly.

4 Repot in the terracotta pots using some of the gritty soil mix to set it in firmly. Water immediately and frequently when they are on display. Auriculas do best in sun or partial shade.

Terracotta Planter of Spring Bulbs

This container of bright yellow tulips and daffodils will brighten the dullest spring day. The variegated ivies conceal the soil and pleasantly soften the edge of the planter.

MATERIALS AND TOOLS
Terracotta planter, 60 cm (24 in) long
Crocks or similar drainage material
Standard soil mix
Trowel

PLANTS
10 tulips
6 pots of miniature daffodils
6 variegated ivies

tulip

miniature daffodil

ivy

1 Fill the bottom of the planter with drainage material. Be especially careful to cover the drainage holes so that they do not become clogged with soil mix.

2 Remove the tulips from their pots and carefully separate the bulbs. Plant them in a staggered double row down the length of the planter.

GARDENER'S TIP

Plant in early spring.

3 Interplant the container with the miniature daffodils.

4 Finally plant the ivies around the edge of the planter. Remember that if you are using a planter like this as a window box, the back of the arrangement should look just as good as the front.

Tinware Planter of Lily-of-the-valley

Lily-of-the-valley grow very well in containers and they will thrive in the shade where their delicate scented flowers stand out amongst the greenery. Surrounding the plants with sheet moss is practical as well as attractive as it will stop the soil splashing back onto the leaves and flowers during spring showers.

MATERIALS AND TOOLS
Tinware planter
Clay granules
Standard soil mix
Sheet moss
Trowel

PLANTS
6–8 pots of lily-of-the-valley

lily-of-the-valley

1 Fill the bottom of the planter with 5 cm (2 in) of clay granules.

2 Cover the granules with a layer of soil mix and place the lily-of-the-valley plants on the soil mix.

3 Fill in around the plants with more soil mix, making sure to press firmly around the plants so that they won't rock about in the wind. Now cover the soil with sheet moss, fitting it snugly around the stems of the lily-of-the-valley, as the moss will help keep the plants upright.

GARDENER'S TIP

If you want to bring your planter indoors to enjoy the scent of the flowers, use a planter without drainage holes in the base, but be very careful not to overwater. Once the plants have finished flowering replant them in a pot with normal drainage holes or in the garden. They are woodland plants and will be quite happy under trees.

Plant in early spring.

Wooden Tub with Daffodils and Wallflowers

A weathered wooden tub planted in the autumn with daffodil bulbs and wallflower plants will provide a colorful spring display. Alternatively you can buy pots of daffodils and wallflowers in bud in the early spring for an instant display.

MATERIALS AND TOOLS
Wooden tub, 35 cm (14 in) diameter
Styrofoam plant tray
Standard soil mix
Slow-release plant food granules
Trowel

PLANTS
24 daffodil bulbs or 4 × 1 litre (5 in) pots of daffodils
3 bushy wallflower (*Cheiranthus*) plants

daffodils

wallflower

1 Break the styrofoam tray into large pieces and fill the bottom third of the tub to provide drainage and save on the quantity of soil mix used.

2 Add soil mix until the tub is half-full and arrange 12 of the daffodil bulbs evenly over the surface. Cover the bulbs with soil mix.

3 Arrange the other 12 bulbs on the surface of the soil mix.

GARDENER'S TIP

To save the bulbs for next year allow the leaves to die right back and then dig up and store in a cool dry place.

Plant bulbs in the autumn or plants in bud in spring.

4 Remove the wallflower plants from their pots and place them on the soil mix. Don't worry if the plants cover some of the bulbs, they will grow around the wallflowers. Fill the tub with soil mix, pressing down firmly around the wallflowers to ensure that they do not work loose in windy weather. Sprinkle a tablespoon of slow-release plant granules onto the surface and work into the top 3 cm (1 in) of soil mix.

Woodland Garden

You don't need your own woodland area for this garden, just a shady corner and an attractive container to hold a selection of plants that thrive in damp shade. The plants are buried in bark chippings in their pots and will relish these conditions as they imitate their natural habitat so closely.

MATERIALS AND TOOLS
Glazed pot, 50 cm (20 in) diameter
Bark chippings
Scoop or trowel

PLANTS
Pot of bluebells
3 hardy ferns with contrasting shape and color foliage
Pot of *Anemone blanda*

Anemone blanda

fern

bluebells

GARDENER'S TIP

After the bluebells and anemones have finished flowering lift them out of the container in their pots and set them aside in a shady corner to rest. They can be replaced by other woodland plants such as wild strawberries or periwinkles.

Plant in early spring.

1 Fill the container three-quarters full with bark.

2 Plant your largest pot (in this case the bluebells) first. Simply scoop a hollow in the bark and position the plants so that the base of the leaves is approximately 5 cm (2 in) below the rim of the pot.

3 Cover the pot with bark so that the plastic is no longer visible and the plant is surrounded by chippings.

4 Add the ferns, trying them in different positions until you are happy with the way they relate to one another.

5 Fill the spaces between the ferns with bark.

6 Add the *Anemone blanda* at the front of the container where its flowers will be seen to best advantage and then carpet the whole arrangement with bark. Stand the container in light shade and water.

Flowers of Ancient Egypt

The *Agapanthus* is commonly known as the Nile lily, and the blues and golds of this painted pot are reminiscent of the rich colors of Ancient Egypt. The trailing bellflowers soften the outline of the pot.

MATERIALS AND TOOLS
Terracotta pot, 30 cm (12 in) diameter
Paintbrush
Mid-blue stencil paint
Dark blue stencil paint
Fine sandpaper or steel wool
Scrap of soft cloth
Pot or tube of wax gilt (available from art shops)
Crocks
Equal mix loam-based soil mix and container soil mix
Slow-release plant food granules
Trowel

PLANTS
Nile lily (*Agapanthus*)
3 Italian bellflowers (*Campanula isophylla*)

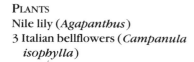

Nile lily

Italian bellflower

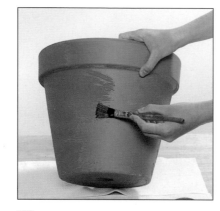

1 Apply a coat of mid-blue paint to the pot. Allow to dry.

2 Apply a coat of the deep blue paint.

3 When it is dry, rub down gently with sandpaper so that some of the lighter blue paint and the terracotta show through.

4 Dip the soft cloth in the wax gilt and apply at random to the pot to create a burnished effect.

5 Place some crocks over the drainage hole at the bottom of the pot. Plant the Nile lily, filling round the edges of the rootball with soil mix.

GARDENER'S TIP

If you would like a more dramatic and architectural effect, mulch around the Nile lily with stones that have been sprayed gold instead of planting the bellflowers.

Plant in early summer.

6 Plant the bellflowers around the edges of the pot, firming the plants in gently. Scatter a tablespoon of slow-release plant food granules on the surface of the soil mix. Water and position in full sun. The Nile lily will benefit from winter protection.

Chinese Water Garden

In China these glazed pots are frequently used as small ponds in courtyards. This pot contains a water lily, a flowering rush and an arum lily.

MATERIALS AND TOOLS
Glazed pot, at least 70 cm (28 in) diameter
Water lily basket
Piece of burlap
Large bucket
aquatic soil mix
Putty (optional)
Bricks

PLANTS
Compact water lily (*Nymphaea pygmaea* 'Alba' was used here)
Flowering rush (*Butomus umbellatus*)
Arum lily (*Zantedeschia aethiopica*)

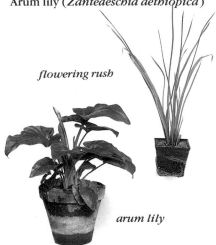

flowering rush

arum lily

water lily

1 Line the lily basket with the burlap.

2 Gently place the water lily in the lined pot.

3 Carefully fill the lily basket with aquatic soil mix.

GARDENER'S TIP

This arrangement is not recommended for anyone with small children; they can drown in a surprisingly small amount of water.

Plant in late spring or early summer.

4 Lower the planted water lily into a bucket of water to settle the soil mix.

5 If the glazed pot has a drainage hole, block it off with putty and leave it to harden overnight. The plants need to be placed at different levels in the water. Use bricks to create platforms within the pot, leaving one corner without bricks for the water lily.

6 Before filling the pot with water, position the rush so that its pot will be fully submerged and the arum lily so that its pot will be half submerged.

7 Fill the pot with water and gently lower the water lily into position – its leaves should float on the surface. This water garden will do best in a sunny position.

Regency Lily Urn

The shape of this urn is based on the shape of the lily flower, so it makes an appropriate container for this lovely mix of lilies, lavenders, pink marguerites and *Helichrysum*.

MATERIALS AND TOOLS
Suitably shaped urn
Gravel
Loam-based soil mix with
   ⅓ added grit
Slow-release plant food granules
Trowel

PLANTS
2 white lilies
2 dwarf lavender ('Hidcote' was used here)
2 pink marguerites
3 *Helichrysum petiolatum*

lily

lavender

marguerite

Helichrysum petiolatum

1 Place a 5 cm (2 in) layer of gravel at the bottom of the urn and half-fill the container with soil mix. Place the lilies in the center of the container.

2 Arrange the lavenders and marguerites around the lilies.

3 Plant the *Helichrysum* around the edge of the urn so that they can cascade over the rim as they grow. Fill between the plants with additional soil mix enriched with a tablespoon of slow-release plant food granules. Water well and place in a sunny position

GARDENER'S TIP

Cut back the lavender heads when they have finished flowering, leave the lilies to die down naturally and dead-head the marguerites regularly to keep them flowering all summer. The *Helichrysum* and marguerites are not frost hardy, but the lavender and lilies should bloom again next year.

Plant in spring to flower in summer.

Shady Corner

Shady corners are often thought of as problematical, when in fact there is a wealth of wonderful plants that thrive in these situations, such as the hosta, hydrangea and fern used in this arrangement.

MATERIALS AND TOOLS
3 terracotta pots of various sizes
Crocks
Composted manure
Equal mix standard soil mix and loam-
    based soil mix
Trowel

PLANTS
Hosta sieboldiana elegans
Variegated hydrangea
Polystichum fern

Hosta sieboldiana elegans

*variegated
hydrangea*

Polystichum *fern*

1 Plant the hosta in a pot large enough for its bulky root system and with space for further growth. The pot used here nicely echoes the shape of the leaves. Place crocks at the bottom of the pot and then a layer of manure before adding the potting soil mix. Follow this procedure with the hydrangea as well.

2 Plant the fern in a terracotta pot slightly larger than its existing pot. It should not need transplanting for two to three years.

3 The hydrangea makes a great deal of growth during the summer and will get very top heavy. Plant in a pot with plenty of space for root growth and heavy enough to prevent the plant toppling over.

GARDENER'S TIP

The hosta is a beautiful foliage plant much loved by slugs and snails which chew unsightly holes in the leaves. To prevent this, smear an inch-wide band of petroleum jelly below the rim of the container and the leaves will remain untouched.

Plant at any time of the year.

Seaside Garden

Even if you live miles from the sea you can create your own seaside garden in a sunny corner with some seashells, succulents and driftwood.

MATERIALS AND TOOLS
4 terracotta pots of various sizes
Seashells
Self-hardening clay
Loam-based soil mix with
⅓ added grit
Gravel
Driftwood
Trowel

PLANTS
Gazania
3 *Mesembryanthemum*
2 *Crassula*
Upright *Lampranthus*
2 trailing *Lampranthus*

Gazania

Lampranthus

1 Fill the back of the shells with clay, leaving some unfilled to cover the soil.

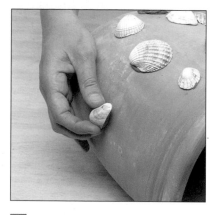

2 Press the shells onto the terracotta pots and leave the clay to harden overnight.

3 Plant the *Gazania* in one of the larger pots.

4 Plant the *Mesembryanthemum* as a group in one pot.

GARDENER'S TIP

Seaside plants are used to growing in difficult surroundings. Be careful not to kill them with too much kindness, and be especially careful not to overwater.

Plant in late spring or early summer.

5 Plant the *Crassula* together in a fairly small pot. These plants grow naturally in poor soils and do not mind a bit of overcrowding.

6 The upright and trailing *Lampranthus* have similar color foliage and flowers, but are quite different shapes so they make an interesting contrast when planted together. Cover the soil of each pot with a layer of gravel and then add seashells and pieces of driftwood. Group together in a sunny position.

Mediterranean Garden

The brilliant colors of the Mediterranean are re-created with these painted pots. The plants thrive in the climate of the Mediterranean, but will also perform well in less predictable weather.

MATERIALS AND TOOLS
4 terracotta pots of various sizes
Paintbrush
Selection of brightly colored emulsion
  paints
Masking tape
Crocks
Loam-based soil mix with
  ⅓ added grit
Gravel

PLANTS
Prostrate rosemary
Aloe
Golden thyme
Large red geranium

geranium

aloe

prostrate rosemary

golden thyme

1 Paint the pots with solid colors or with patterns. The paints used here are thicker than ordinary emulsion, so you may need two coats to get the same effect. The terracotta absorbs the moisture from the paint, so they will dry very quickly.

2 Paint the rim of one pot with a contrasting color.

3 Create a pattern using tape to mask out specific areas.

4 Paint every other area to create a zig-zag effect.

5 Place crocks in the bottom of the pots and then position the plants, firming them in place with extra soil mix. The roots of this rosemary are compacted and will benefit from being teased loose before planting.

GARDENER'S TIP

For commercial reasons the plants you buy will probably have been grown in a peat soil mix, although they prefer a loam-based soil mix. Gently loosen the peat around their roots and mix it with the loam-based soil mix before potting them up in the new mixture.

Plant in late spring or early summer.

6 The aloe does not need a large pot. Plant it in a pot just slightly larger than the one you bought it in.

7 Plant the thyme and geranium in separate pots. Finish the plants with a top-dressing of gravel, water well and place in a sheltered sunny corner.

Hen-and-chicks Bowl

These wonderfully textured low-growing plants hug the surface of the gravel to create an unusual planted bowl. These plants can grow in very poor soils and in this instance are planted in gravel instead of soil mix.

MATERIALS AND TOOLS
Pottery or stone bowl, 25 cm (10 in) diameter, with drainage holes
Washed gravel

PLANTS
2 hen-and-chicks (*Sempervivum*)
Saxifraga paniculata

hen-and-chick

Saxifraga paniculata

1 Half-fill the bowl with gravel.

2 Remove the plants from their pots. Position the largest plant first – it may be necessary to scoop out some of the gravel underneath it. If it is a hen-and-chicks with small rosettes hanging from it in tendrils (like the one used here), arrange these so they hang over the edge of the bowl.

3 Position the *saxifraga* next to the other plant, so that the gravel is level with its bottom row of leaves.

4 Add the final plant and top off with more gravel if necessary. Water and place in full sun.

GARDENER'S TIP

Hen-and-chicks propagate very freely. Simply remove small-rooted rosettes and pot up in an equal mix of soil-based soil mix and grit.

Plant in late spring or early summer.

Foliage Basket

An old basket makes an ideal container for this interesting group of foliage plants. The different leaf shapes and colors are emphasized when they are grouped together. The addition of flowers would detract from the architectural quality of the plants.

MATERIALS AND TOOLS
Basket, 30 cm (12 in) diameter
Sphagnum moss
Loam-based soil mix
Slow-release plant food granules
Bark mulch

PLANTS
Phormium tenax
Mexican orange blossom
(*Choisya ternata*)
Carex brunnea 'Variegata'

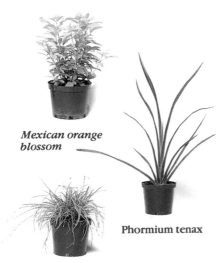

Mexican orange blossom

Phormium tenax

Carex brunnea 'Variegata'

GARDENER'S TIP

A planted basket makes an ideal gift for a friend, especially when you have chosen the plants yourself. Include a label, giving the names of the plants and how to care for them.

Plant at any time of the year.

1 Line the basket with moss to prevent the soil leaking out.

2 Place the *Phormium* at the back of the basket and position the *Choisya* next to it.

3 Add the *Carex* 'Variegata' and fill between the plants with soil mix enriched with a tablespoon of slow-release plant food granules.

4 Mulch around the plants with bark. Water well and place in partial shade.

Wild Strawberry Basket

Wild strawberries can be grown in a basket and enjoyed anywhere, whether in the countryside or a small city garden.

MATERIALS
Wire basket, 30 cm (12 in) square
Sphagnum moss
Equal mix loam-based soil mix and
    container soil mix
Slow-release plant food granules
Trowel

PLANTS
4 Alpine strawberry plants

**Alpine strawberry
plant**

1 Line the basket with a generous layer of sphagnum moss.

2 Fill the lined area with soil mix. Scoop out a hollow for each strawberry plant, and press the soil mix firmly around the rootball as you plant.

3 Some of the plants may already be sending out runners. Make sure these hang over the edge of the basket so that as they grow they can be used to grow extra plants (see Gardener's Tip).

GARDENER'S TIP

Propagate strawberry runners by pinning the plantlets into small pots of soil mix. A loop of wire or a hairpin either side of the plantlet will hold it firmly in place until it has rooted. Then simply cut the runner and you have a new, free strawberry plant.

Plant in spring to fruit in summer.

4 Scatter a tablespoon of plant food granules on the surface of the soil mix.

5 Tuck more moss around the edges of the basket and under the leaves of the plants. This will conserve moisture and stop the fruit touching the soil. Water and place in full or partial sun.

Butler's Tray Kitchen Garden

Not many of us have the space or time to maintain a kitchen garden, but this table-top selection of plants will give you a taste of the delights to be had, and might even inspire you to try the real thing.

MATERIALS AND TOOLS
Terracotta pots of various sizes
Crocks
Standard soil mix
Butler's tray
Thick plastic sheet
Clay granules
Trowel

PLANTS
Selection of kitchen garden plants, such as marigold, basil, nasturtium, miniature tomato, strawberry and tarragon

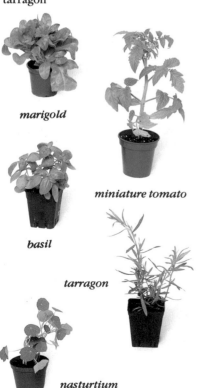

marigold

miniature tomato

basil

tarragon

nasturtium

GARDENER'S TIP
The marigolds and nasturtiums are not purely decorative; the flowers of both plants and the leaves of the nasturtium are edible and can be used in salads.

Plant in late spring or early summer.

1 Place crocks in the bottom of the pots for drainage.

2 This marigold has a well-developed root system which will benefit from planting into a larger pot. Gently squeeze the rootball and tease loose some of the roots before you repot the plant.

3 Divide a single pot of basil into two or more pots when repotting.

4 Nasturtiums flower better in poor soil. Once you have planted them, leave them to their own devices. Give them a little water but no plant food or you will get lots of leaves and very few flowers.

5 The miniature tomato and the strawberry should be planted in larger pots to allow plenty of room for root development. The tarragon should be planted in a pot slightly larger than the one it was bought in. Line your tray with a thick plastic sheet and cover this with clay granules. These retain moisture and create a damp microclimate for the plants. Arrange your plants on the tray, place in a sunny position and water and feed (except the nasturtiums) regularly.

Summer Flower Basket

The secret of a successful wall or hanging basket is to be generous with the plants. The result will then be a marvelous display of color which will last all summer long.

MATERIALS AND TOOLS
Wall basket, 30 cm (12 in) diameter
Terracotta or plastic pot (optional)
Sphagnum moss
Hanging basket soil mix
Slow-release plant food granules

PLANTS
6 lilac lobelia
3 pink petunias
2 *Convolvulus mauritanicus*
2 blue petunias
Lilac lantana
Trailing geranium

1 Rest your basket on a pot. This will hold it upright and allow you to work more easily.

2 Line the base of the basket and one-third of the way up the sides with a thick layer of moss.

lobelia

lantana

petunia

3 Fill the moss-lined area with soil mix and plant four of the lobelia through the sides of the basket, so that their rootballs rest on the soil mix.

4 Add another layer of moss and soil mix, firming the remaining lobelias in as you work.

5 Just below the rim of the basket plant a pink petunia centrally with the *Convolvulus* at either side. Again introduce the plants through the sides of the basket.

Convolvulus mauritanicus

GARDENER'S TIP

If you are going away for a week or two, move your baskets and container plants into a cool shady corner of the garden and water copiously before you leave. In cool weather they should stay in good condition until your return, and in hot weather your neighbors will only need to check them twice a week instead of daily.

Plant in late spring or early summer.

6 Add a further layer of moss and soil mix above these plants and plant the remaining petunias, the lantana and the geranium in the top of the basket, firming down well as you plant them. Scatter a tablespoon of plant food granules over the surface of the soil mix. This will feed the plants throughout the growing season. Water well before hanging the basket in a sunny position and then water daily in the morning or evening.

Potted Fruit Garden

Dwarf apple trees grow well in containers provided they are fed and watered regularly. With the addition of strawberry plants around the base of the apple tree you will be able to enjoy two crops of fruit from your potted garden. The strawberry plants are kept in their pots and bedded down in bark mulch as fruit trees don't like to compete for soil space.

MATERIALS AND TOOLS
Terracotta pot, 60 cm (24 in) high
Crocks or similar drainage material
Composted stable manure
Knife
Bonemeal
Loam-based soil mix
Bark mulch
Trowel

PLANTS
Apple tree on dwarf rooting stock
5 strawberry plants

1 Cover the drainage holes in the base of the pot with crocks or similar drainage material and a 10 cm (4 in) layer of composted manure.

strawberry plant

GARDENER'S TIP
Standard gooseberries and redcurrants also grow well in containers and look highly decorative when they are fruiting.

Plant in autumn or spring to fruit in summer.

2 Use a knife to cut the plastic pot away from the tree rather than pulling the pot off, which can damage the rootball.

3 Place the tree in the pot and scatter a handful of bonemeal around the rootball. Then add the loam-based soil mix, filling the pot to approximately 10 cm (4 in) below the rim.

4 Place the strawberry plants in their pots around the trunk of the tree and fill the spaces in between with bark mulch. Place in a sunny position, and water and liquid feed regularly.

Scented Window Box

The soft silvers and blues of the flowers and foliage beautifully complement this verdigris window box. The scent of the lavender and petunias will drift magically through open windows.

MATERIALS AND TOOLS
Window box, 60 cm (24 in) long
Gravel or similar drainage material
Equal mix loam-based soil mix and
   container soil mix
Slow-release plant food granules

PLANTS
2 lavender
2 pale blue petunias
3 deep blue petunias
3 *Chaenorrhinum glareosum* (lilac
   lobelia may be used instead)
6 *Helichrysum petiolare*

lavender

Chaenorrhinum
glareosum

petunia

petunia

I Fill the bottom 5 cm (2 in) of the window box with drainage material and then half-fill with a layer of soil mix. Position the lavender plants, loosening the soil around the roots before planting, as they will establish better this way.

2 Now arrange the flowering plants around the lavender, leaving spaces for the *Helichrysum* between them.

3 Finally add the foliage plants and fill between the plants with soil mix, pressing firmly so that no air gaps are left around the roots. Place in a sunny position and water regularly.

GARDENER'S TIP

To keep a densely planted container like this looking its best it is necessary to feed regularly with a liquid feed, or more simply to mix slow-release fertilizer granules into the surface of the soil mix to last the whole summer. Cut back the lavender heads after flowering to ensure a bushy flowering plant again next year.

Plant in late spring or early summer.

Star-jasmine in a Villandry Planter

The soft, seductive scent of the star-jasmine makes this a perfect container to be placed by the side of a door where the scent will be appreciated by all who pass through.

MATERIALS AND TOOLS
Villandry planter or similar, approx 50 cm (18 in) square, preferably self-watering
Equal mix loam-based soil mix and standard soil mix
Slow-release plant food granules
Bark mulch
Trowel

PLANTS
Star-jasmine (*Trachelospermum jasminoides*)

star-jasmine

GARDENER'S TIP

Use a plastic liner inside all large planters. It is easier to remove the liner when replanting rather than to replant the entire container.

Plant in late spring or early summer.

1 Feed wicks through the holes in the base of the liner.

2 Fill the water reservoir in the base of the planter to the top of the overflow pipe and place the liner inside the planter.

3 Fill the bottom of the liner with soil mix while pulling through the wicks so that they reach the level of the jasmine roots.

4 Remove the jasmine from its pot, gently tease the roots loose and stand it in the planter.

Note Steps 1–3 are for a self-watering planter only.

5 Add soil mix and firm it around the rootball of the jasmine. Scatter 2 tablespoons of plant food granules on the surface and gently work it into the top layer of soil mix with the trowel.

6 Mulch around the plant with a layer of bark, then water. Check the reservoir of the self-watering container once a week and top up if necessary. Conventional pots should be watered daily in the early morning or evening during hot weather.

Galvanized Bath Garden

An old tin bath makes an ideal planter; it is large and deep enough to take quite large plants. Here, foxgloves and euphorbia are underplanted with violets, making an attractive early summer display.

MATERIALS AND TOOLS
Tin bath, 60 cm (24 in) wide
Gravel or similar drainage material
Equal mix loam-based soil mix and
    standard soil mix
Slow-release plant food granules
Trowel

PLANTS
3 foxgloves (*Digitalis*)
2 euphorbia
3 violets

euphorbia

foxglove

violets

1 If the bath does not have drainage holes, you should make some in the base, and then cover it with a 10 cm (4 in) layer of gravel or similar drainage material. Half-fill the bath with the soil mix, and position the foxgloves.

2 Next add the euphorbia, teasing loose the roots to enable growth if they are at all potbound. Fill between the plants with soil mix, pressing down firmly around the rootballs.

3 Finally plant the violets around the edges, where they can tumble over the sides as they grow. Water and place in a shady position.

GARDENER'S TIP

Buy your foxgloves before they have formed their flower spikes; they will transplant better and you will have the pleasure of watching them grow. Don't cut the stems down after flowering; leave them to ripen on the plant, and when you can hear the seeds rattling, simply shake them over any corner of the garden where you would like foxgloves to grow.

Plant in autumn or spring to flower in summer.

Chimney Pot Clematis

It is well known that clematis love to have their heads in the sun and their roots in the shade. A chimney pot creates the perfect environment as it provides exactly these conditions. Ideally the clematis should be planted in soil with the chimney pot placed over it, but with a little care and attention, pot-grown plants will do well for a few years.

MATERIALS AND TOOLS
Chimney pot, 60 cm (24 in) high
2 plastic pots, 20 cm (8 in) diameter
Gravel
Equal mix loam-based soil mix and
    container soil mix
Slow-release plant food granules

PLANTS
Clematis ('Prince Charles' was used
    here)

clematis

1 Fill one of the plastic pots with gravel.

2 Plant your clematis in the other plastic pot, filling around the rootball with the soil mix. Scatter a tablespoon of plant food granules over the surface of the soil mix. (The two pots will be positioned one on top of the other inside the chimney pot, as shown.)

3 Place the chimney pot over the pot of gravel and then carefully lower the clematis pot into position. It will need a sunny position and regular watering.

GARDENER'S TIP

Clematis can suffer from clematis wilt: suddenly whole stems will start to wilt and die. Cut all affected parts away from the plant and spray the remaining plant every two weeks with a product containing Benomyl.

Plant in spring to flower in summer.

LATE SUMMER AND AUTUMN CONTAINERS

Autumn Color

Long Tom pots were very popular in Victorian times. They are now being made again and are available in a variety of colors. There is a wonderfully architectural quality to the outline of this cream Long Tom and the plants it contains.

MATERIALS AND TOOLS
Long Tom, 30 cm (12 in) diameter
Crocks
Equal mix loam-based soil mix and
    standard soil mix
Clay saucer
Gravel
Slow-release plant food granules
Trowel or scoop

PLANTS
Cape figwort (*Phygelius*)
Day lily (*Hemerocallis dumortieri*)
Hardy fuchsia, preferably a variety
    with compact growth

day lily

Cape figwort

fuchsia

GARDENER'S TIP
These plants will look marvelous for one season, but after that they will benefit from being repotted into a larger container.

Plant in spring or early summer to flower in autumn.

1 Cover the drainage holes at the base of the pot with crocks.

2 Position the largest plant first. You will probably have to loosen the soil around the rootballs of the plants to fit them all in the pot. Gently squeeze the soil and tease the roots loose.

3 Add the other two plants, again loosening the soil if necessary.

4 Fill any spaces between the plants with soil mix, and push the soil mix firmly down the sides of the pot so that no air spaces are left.

5 The shape of the container means that the soil will dry out quite quickly, especially when so densely planted. To counteract this, stand it in a clay saucer filled with wet gravel.

6 Scatter 1 tablespoon of plant food granules onto the soil mix and mix in. Water regularly and place in a sunny position.

Pot of Sunflowers

Sunflowers grow very well in pots provided you are not growing the giant varieties. Grow your own from seed; there are many kinds to choose from, including the double flowers used here.

MATERIALS AND TOOLS
Large glazed pot, 30 cm (12 in) diameter
Styrofoam or similar drainage material
Equal mix loam-based soil mix and container soil mix
Slow-release plant food granules

PLANTS
3 strong sunflower seedlings, approximately 20 cm (8 in) tall

sunflower seedling

1 Line the base of the pot with drainage material.

2 Fill the pot with the soil mix, pressing down so that there are no air spaces. Scoop out evenly spaced holes for each seedling and plant, firming the soil mix around the plants.

3 Scatter 1 tablespoon of plant food granules on the surface of the soil mix. Place in a sunny position, out of the wind, and water regularly.

GARDENER'S TIP

Allow at least one of the sunflower heads to set seed. As the plant starts to die back, cut off the seedhead and hang it upside-down to ripen. Reserve some seeds for next year and then hang the seedhead outside for the birds.

Plant seeds in spring and small seedlings in summer to flower in late summer.

Colorful Cooking Pot

Junk shops are a rich source of old pots and pans which can make characterful containers for plants when their kitchen days are over.

MATERIALS AND TOOLS
Cooking pot, 30 cm (12 in) diameter
Gravel
Equal mix loam-based soil mix and container soil mix
Slow-release plant food granules
Trowel

PLANTS
Ceratostigma plumbaginoides
Inula ('Oriental star' was used here)
Golden ivy

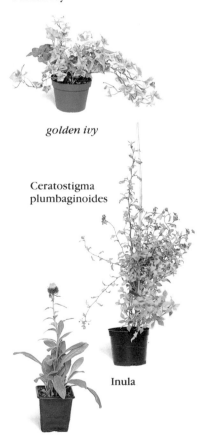

golden ivy

Ceratostigma plumbaginoides

Inula

1 If the pot doesn't already have some holes in the base, make one or two for drainage. Fill the bottom of the pot with a 5 cm (2 in) layer of gravel.

2 Remove the *Ceratostigma* from its pot and plant it at one side of the pot.

3 Add the *Inula* and the ivy, and fill between the plants with soil mix, firming them in position as you work. Scatter a tablespoon of plant food granules over the surface of the soil mix. Water and place in a sunny position.

GARDENER'S TIP

These plants are all perennials. When the *Ceratostigma* and *Inula* have finished flowering, plant them in a border in the garden where they will flower again next year.

Plant in spring or early summer to flower in late summer.

Alpine Sink

An old stone sink is a perfect container for a collection of Alpine plants. The rock helps create the effect of a miniature landscape and provides shelter for some of the plants. The sink is set up on the stand of an old sewing machine so that the beauty of the tiny plants can be admired easily.

MATERIALS AND TOOLS
A stone sink or trough,
  75 cm × 50 cm (30 in × 20 in)
Crocks
Moss-covered rock
Loam-based soil mix with ⅓ added
  coarse grit
Washed gravel
Trowel

PLANTS
Achillea tomentosa
Veronica penduncularis
Ivy
Sedum spathulifolium purpureum
Hebe
Sedum ewersii
Aster natalensis
Alpine willow (*Salix alpina*)
Arabis ferdinandi-coburgii
  'Variegata'

2 Position the rock. It is important to do this before adding the soil to create the effect of a natural rocky outcrop. This will never be achieved if you place your rock onto the surface of the soil mix.

3 Pour the soil mix into the sink. (If you are lucky enough to have a moss-covered sink, like the one used here, be careful not to disturb the moss or cover it with soil mix.)

1 Cover the drainage hole of the sink with crocks.

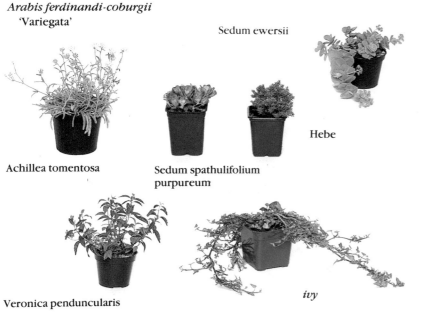

Sedum ewersii

Hebe

Achillea tomentosa

Sedum spathulifolium
purpureum

Veronica penduncularis

ivy

4 Plan the positions of your plants so that the end result will have a good balance of shape and color. Start planting from one end. As the sink is very shallow you will need to scoop out the soil right to the base before planting. Alpine plants are used to shallow soil so this will not cause any problems.

GARDENER'S TIP

If you do not have a stone sink you could use a butler's sink instead. You could even give it a stone effect by covering it with a mix of Portland cement, sand and peat in proportions of 1 to 2.5 to 1.5. You will need to cover the whole surface with impact bonding PVA glue before applying the mix to the sink. Build up the layers gradually, wearing rubber gloves.

Plant in spring to flower in autumn.

5 Be careful to ensure that the bottom leaves of low-growing plants are level with the soil. Too low and they will rot; too high and they will dry out.

6 When all the plants are in place, carefully pour washed gravel all around them, lifting leaves to cover the whole soil area. Water and place in full or partial sun.

Autumn Hanging Basket

Towards the end of summer the colors of traditional hanging baskets do not always marry happily with the reds and golds of autumn. This is the time to plant a richly colored hanging basket for winter.

MATERIALS AND TOOLS
Hanging basket, 30 cm (12 in) diameter
Plastic pot
Sphagnum moss
Equal mix loam-based soil mix and standard soil mix
Slow-release plant food granules
Trowel

PLANTS
6 winter-flowering pansies
3 variegated ivies
Euonymus fortunei ('Emerald and Gold' was used here)
2 dahlias (optional)

dahlia

winter-flowering pansy

variegated ivy

Euonymus fortunei

1 Support the hanging basket on a pot. Unhook the chain from one fixing point so that it hangs down one side of the basket. Line the base and bottom half of the basket with a generous layer of sphagnum moss.

2 Pour in soil mix until it is level with the top of the moss. Plant your first layer of three pansies and three ivies, passing the foliage through the bars of the basket, so that the rootballs of the plants are resting on the soil mix.

3 Line the rest of the basket with moss, fill up with soil mix, firming it around the roots of the ivies and pansies, and then plant the remaining plants in the top of the basket, with the *Euonymus* in the center and the pansies and dahlias surrounding it. Scatter a tablespoon of slow-release plant food granules onto the soil mix and water the hanging basket well. Re-attach the chain and hang the basket in full or partial sun.

GARDENER'S TIP

Although special hanging basket soil mixes with water-retaining gel are a boon for summer containers and hanging baskets, they can be too moist for the damper, cooler months of the year and tend to get waterlogged. Mix equal parts loam-based soil mix with a standard soil mix for good free-draining results for autumn and winter planting.

Plant in spring or summer to flower in autumn.

Heather Window Box

This is a perfect project for an absolute beginner as it is extremely simple to achieve. The bark window box is a sympathetic container for the heathers, which look very much at home in their bed of moss.

MATERIALS AND TOOLS
Bark window box, 30 cm (12 in) long
Crocks or similar drainage material
Ericaceous soil mix
Sheet moss

PLANTS
3 heathers

heathers

GARDENER'S TIP

Do not be tempted to use ordinary soil mix as it contains lime, which, with a very few exceptions, is not suitable for the majority of heathers.

Plant in autumn.

1 Put a layer of crocks or similar drainage material in the bottom of the box.

2 Remove the heathers from their pots and position them in the window box.

3 Fill the gaps between the plants with the soil mix, pressing it around the plants. Water.

4 Tuck the sheet moss snugly around the plants so that no soil is visible. Place in sun or partial sun.

Black and White Arrangement

Customize your container with paint to match your choice of plants. Here, dramatic black and white was used to great effect, providing a real focal point in the garden.

MATERIALS AND TOOLS
Terracotta pot, 30 cm (12 in) high
Masking tape
Paintbrush
Matt white paint
Matt black paint (if you don't want it to weather, use eggshell)
Crocks
Standard soil mix
Slow-release plant food granules
2 packets of cactus gravel or similar fine gravel
Trowel

PLANTS
White *Osteospermum*
Black grass (*Ophiopogon nigrescens*)
3 violets (*Viola* 'Molly Sanderson' was used here)

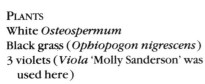
Osteospermum

black grass

violet

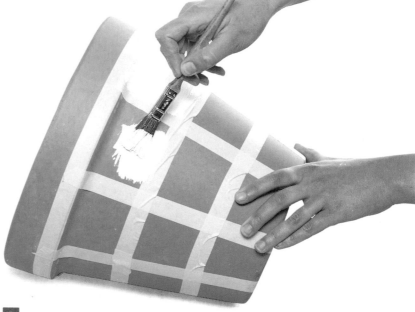

1 Mark out the checkered pattern onto the pot with masking tape.

2 Paint the top and bottom row of checks white.

3 Paint the rim of the pot and the middle row black.

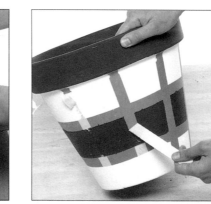

4 Gently peel off the masking tape.

5 Cover the drainage holes at the bottom of the pot with crocks and half-fill with soil mix. Remove the *Osteospermum* from its pot, gently tease out its roots and position it at the back of the container.

GARDENER'S TIP

Experiment with other color themes. You could try a sky blue and white check container planted with a morning glory.

Plant in spring or early summer to flower in late summer.

6 Place the black grass next to the *Osteospermum* and fill up the container with soil mix, firming around the plants. Plant the three violets in a group, again being careful to firm them in place. Scatter a tablespoon of plant food granules on the surface of the soil mix.

7 Mulch around the plants with the fine gravel, and water. These plants need to be in a sunny position.

Gothic Ivy

Twisted willow branches set into a chimney pot
offer an attractive support for ivy and will provide
welcome interest in the winter.

MATERIALS AND TOOLS
Chimney pot
Standard soil mix
1 m (1 yard) wire netting

PLANTS
4 or 5 branches of twisted willow
Large ivy (*Hedera helix* var. *hibernica*
was used here)

ivy

1 Place the chimney pot in its final position (in shade or half-shade) and half fill with soil mix. Fold or crumple the wire netting and push down into the chimney pot so that it rests on the soil mix.

2 Arrange the willow branches in the chimney pot, pushing the stems through the wire netting so that they stay in place.

3 Rest the ivy, in its pot, on the wire netting amongst the willow branches. Fill the chimney pot with soil mix to within 10 cm (4 in) of the rim.

4 Carefully cut loose any ties and remove the supporting stake.

GARDENER'S TIP

You may find that some of your twisted willow branches take root in the soil mix. Plant a rooted branch in the garden where it will grow into a tree. It will eventually be quite large so don't plant it near the house.

Plant at any time of the year.

5 Arrange the stems of ivy over the willow branches and water. To start with it may look rather contrived, but as the ivy settles to its new surroundings it will attach itself to the willow.

Classic Topiary

The clean lines of the topiary are matched by the simplicity of the terracotta pots. The eye is drawn to the outlines of the box plants so decorated pots would be an unneccesary distraction.

MATERIALS AND TOOLS
4 large terracotta pots
Bark mulch
Crocks
Equal mix loam-based soil mix and
    standard soil mix
Slow-release plant food granules
Trowel

PLANTS
4 box trees (*Buxus*) in different
    topiary shapes

three-ball topiary

corkscrew topiary

ball topiary

1 If the plant has been well looked after in the nursery it may not need potting on yet. In this case simply slip the plant in its pot into the terracotta container.

2 To conserve moisture and conceal the plastic pot, cover with a generous layer of bark.

3 To repot a box tree, first place a good layer of crocks in the bottom of the pot.

4 Remove the tree from its plastic pot and place it in the terracotta pot. Surround the rootball with soil mix.

5 Push the soil mix down the side of the pot to ensure that there are no air spaces.

6 Scatter a tablespoon of plant food granules on the surface of the pot and then top with a good layer of bark. Water well and regularly. Position in sun or partial shade.

Trug of Winter Pansies

Winter pansies are wonderfully resilient and will bloom bravely throughout the winter as long as they are regularly deadheaded. This trug may be moved around to provide color wherever it is needed and acts as a perfect antidote to mid-winter gloom.

MATERIALS AND TOOLS
Old wooden trug
Sphagnum moss
Standard soil mix
Slow-release plant food granules
Trowel

PLANTS
15 winter-flowering pansies

winter-flowering pansies

GARDENER'S TIP

Not everyone has an old trug available, but an old basket, colander, or an enamel bread bin could be used instead. Junk shops and flea markets are a great source of containers that are too battered for their original use, but great for planting.

Plant in autumn to flower in winter.

1 Line the trug with a generous layer of sphagnum moss.

2 Fill the moss lining with soil mix.

3 Plant the pansies by starting at one end and filling the spaces between the plants with soil mix as you go. Gently firm each plant into position and add a final layer of soil mix mixed with a tablespoon of plant food granules around the pansies. Water and place in a fairly sunny position.

Evergreen Garden

Evergreen plants come in many shapes, sizes and shades of green. Grouped together in containers they will provide you with year-round interest and color.

MATERIALS AND TOOLS
Terracotta containers of various sizes
Crocks or similar drainage material
Equal mix loam-based soil mix and
    container soil mix
Saucers
Gravel
Trowel

PLANTS
False cypress (*Chamaecyparis*)
Silver *Euonymus*
Darwin's barberry (*Berberis*
    darwinnii)
Barberry (*Berberis atropurpurea*
    nana)
Cypress (*Cupressus filifera aurea*)
Pachysandra terminalis
Bergenia

barberry

Bergenia

Pachysandra
terminalis

1 Large plants, such as *Chamaecyparis*, should be potted into a proportionally large container. If it is at all potbound, tease the roots loose before planting in its new pot. Place plenty of crocks or similar drainage material at the base of the pot. Fill around the rootball with soil mix, pressing it down firmly around the edges of the pot.

2 Smaller plants, like *Bergenia*, should be planted in a pot slightly larger than its existing pot. Place crocks in the base of the pot, position the plant and then fill around the edges with soil mix.

3 Plants will stay moist longer if they are stood in saucers of wet gravel. This group of plants will do well positioned in partial shade. Water regularly and feed with slow-release plant food granules in the spring and autumn.

GARDENER'S TIP
Include some golden or variegated foliage amongst your evergreens or the group will look rather dull and one dimensional. Experiment for yourself and see how the lighter colors "lift" a group of plants.

Plant at any time of the year.

Golden Christmas Holly

Evergreen standard holly trees are splendid container plants. This golden holly has been dressed up for Christmas with bows and baubles in a gilded pot.

MATERIALS AND TOOLS
Terracotta pot, 40 cm (16 in) high
Gold spray-paint
Crocks or similar drainage material
Composted manure
Loam-based soil mix
Pine cones
1 m (1 yard) wired gold-mesh ribbon, for bow
Selection of tin Christmas decorations, sprayed gold

PLANTS
Golden holly

golden holly

1 Spray the pot with gold paint and leave to dry.

2 Place a good layer of crocks or other drainage material in the base of the pot.

3 Cover with an 8 cm (3 in) layer of soil mixed manure and a thin layer of loam-based potting soil mix. Remove the holly from its existing container and place in the gilded pot, surround the rootball with soil mix, pressing down firmly to ensure that the tree is firmly planted.

4 Surround the base of the tree with pine cones.

GARDENER'S TIP

In the autumn, plant some corms or Reticulata irises or similar small bulbs in the soil mix surrounding the tree for a delightful spring display.

Plant in autumn, winter or spring.

5 Tie a bow with the ribbon and attach it to the trunk of the tree. Hang the decorations in the branches. Water the tree to settle it in, but don't do this on a frosty day or the water will freeze.

Year-round Window Box

In the same way that a garden has certain plants that provide structure throughout the year, this window box has been planted so that there is always plenty of foliage. Extra color may be introduced each season by including small flowering plants, such as heathers.

MATERIALS AND TOOLS
Window box, 1 m (1 yard) long,
 preferably self-watering
Equal mix loam-based soil mix and
 container soil mix
Slow-release plant food granules
Bark mulch
Trowel

PLANTS
Skimmia rubella
2 *Arundinaria pygmaea*
2 *Cotoneaster conspicuus*
2 periwinkles (*Vinca variegata*)
6 heathers

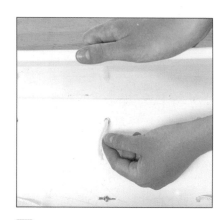

1 Feed the wicks through the base of the plastic liner.

Note: Steps 1 and 2 are for self-watering containers only.

2 Slip the liner into the wooden window box.

3 Before you start planting, plan the positions of the plants so that the colors and shapes look well balanced.

Arundinaria pygmaea

Skimmia rubella

Cotoneaster conspicuus

periwinkle

heather

4 Remove the plants from their pots, tease loose their roots if they look at all potbound and position in the window box. Fill the gaps between the plants with soil mix.

5 Once the structure plants are in place you can add the color, in this case the heathers. Scoop out a hole for each heather and then plant, pressing firmly around each one. Scatter two tablespoons of plant food granules along the surface.

6 Top-dress the window box with a layer of bark; this will help conserve moisture and prevent soil splashes on the leaves. Water.

GARDENER'S TIP

Plants do not need watering in winter, unless they are in a position where the rain does not reach the container. Even then they should be watered sparingly and not in frosty weather. Self-watering containers should be drained before winter to prevent frost damage.

Plant at any time of the year.

Watering Can Planter

An old watering can makes an attractive container, especially when it is painted and stencilled. When planted with an evergreen plant such as the ivy used here, it will provide an eye-catching year-round display.

MATERIALS AND TOOLS
Old watering can
Paintbrush
Eggshell paint, for the base coat
Stencil design
Masking tape
Stencil brush
Stencil paints, for the decoration
Fine paintbrush
Bark mulch
Slow-release plant food granules

PLANTS
Ivy (*Hedera* 'Tres Coupé' was used here)

ivy

1 Paint the watering can with the base color. Apply two coats if necessary and leave each coat to dry thoroughly before painting the next.

2 Fasten the stencil design in place with masking tape. When stencilling, the brush should not hold much paint; dab it on newspaper to get rid of the excess. Use two or three colors to give your design a more three-dimensional effect.

GARDENER'S TIP

Other galvanized tin containers such as tin baths and buckets may also be painted and used for planting.

Plant at any time of the year.

3 Use the fine paintbrush to paint the rim of the can. You could pick out additional detailing if you wish.

4 When all the paint is quite dry, fill the watering can with bark.

5 Scoop out a hollow in the bark and plant the ivy in its pot. Scatter some slow-release plant food granules on the surface. Arrange the tendrils of the ivy so that they trail over the handle and spout of the watering can. Water, pouring any excess water out through the spout. Place the watering can in a shady spot or hang it from a hook in a cool corner.

Orchid Basket

Orchids are no longer the rare exotic plants that they used to be and most garden centers now sell them. A few inexpensive materials and a little time will create a stylish container to show these lovely flowers at their very best.

MATERIALS AND TOOLS
Plastic-lined twig basket, 10 cm (6 in) diameter
Gravel
Sphagnum moss
3 × 40 cm (16 in) stakes
Raffia

PLANTS
Miltonia or *Phalaenopsis* orchid

Miltonia *orchid*

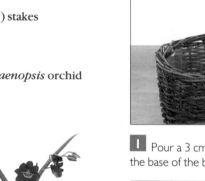

1 Pour a 3 cm (1 in) layer of gravel into the base of the basket.

2 Line the basket with sphagnum moss.

3 Slip the orchid (still in its pot) into the basket.

4 Push the stakes into the moss at the edge of the basket so that they are held firmly in place.

5 Tie a length of raffia between each stake, finishing off with a neat knot.

GARDENER'S TIP

Orchids do not like to stand in water, but they do like a humid atmosphere. A layer of gravel underneath the pot acts as a reservoir for excess water and creates humidity. The orchid will also benefit from being sprayed with water.

Plant at any time of the year.

Plant Crazy

These highly decorative and unusual planters are enhanced by the careful choice of plants which finish the "royal" head-dress. The queen's tresses float delicately above her crown, whilst the king's tumble downwards.

MATERIALS AND TOOLS
2 decorative pots
Gravel
Houseplant soil mix
Trowel

PLANTS
Chandelier plant (*Kalanchoe tubiflora*)
Creeping fig (*Ficus pumila*)

chandelier plant

creeping fig

1 Pour a 5 cm (2 in) layer of gravel into the bottom of the pots.

2 Place the chandelier plant into the planter; if there is any space around the rootball, fill this with houseplant soil mix and gently firm the plant in position.

3 After you have planted the creeping fig, arrange the sprays of leaves so that it resembles hair. As the plant grows it will need an occasional "haircut" to keep it under control. Water regularly and stand in a light position.

GARDENER'S TIP

If you are going away during the summer months, give your houseplants a holiday in the garden. Stand them on a tray lined with a thick layer of damp newspaper, positioned in a shady corner.

Plant at any time of the year.

Citrus Chinoiserie

A miniature citrus tree is a colorful and attractive indoor plant and its scented flowers will fill an entire room with their perfume. A stone mulch is both attractive and practical as it helps prevent moisture evaporating from the soil.

MATERIALS AND TOOLS
Glazed pot, 25 cm (10 in) diameter
Crocks
Equal mix loam-based soil mix and
    container soil mix
Smooth stones

PLANTS
Citrus tree, such as Calamondin
    orange (x *Citrofortunella*)

I Place the crocks in the bottom of the pot.

calamondin orange

2 Position the citrus tree in the pot, being careful not to disturb the rootball. Fill around the tree with soil mix, pressing the soil mix in place.

3 Cover the surface of the soil mix with stones, and water well. Stand in a sunny position. The plant will benefit from being moved outdoors during the summer months.

GARDENER'S TIP

Citrus trees prefer to be repotted in the spring. If you wish to put them in a decorative container at any other time of year, simply use as a cachepot and save repotting for the following spring. When you buy your tree ask for the specialist citrus fertilizers which are now available for summer- and winter-feeding; they are specially formulated and will help keep your tree in the best of health.

Plant in spring.

Indoor Table-top Garden

Many indoor plants and flowers have dramatically colored flowers and foliage. In this arrangement the purple flowers of the African violet are echoed by the velvety leaves of the *Gynura*. The delicate fronds of the maidenhair fern and the dark green foliage of the *Pellaea rotundifolia* add interest with their contrasting shape and color.

GARDENER'S TIP

Terracotta transmits moisture and will mark a table-top if it is in direct contact with it. Cut 2.5 cm (1 in) sections from a cork and glue them to the four corners of the seed tray. A plastic tray smaller than the seed tray can then be slipped underneath it to catch any drips.

Plant at any time of the year.

MATERIALS AND TOOLS
Terracotta seed tray, 30 cm (12 in) wide
Crocks
Houseplant soil mix
Slow-release plant food granules
Clay granules

PLANTS
Maidenhair fern (*Adiantum*)
African violet (*Saintpaulia*)
Gynura
Button-fern (*Pellaea rotundifolia*)

maidenhair fern

African violet

1 Cover the drainage holes in the bottom of the seed tray with crocks.

2 Experiment with how you wish to arrange the plants before removing them from their pots.

3 Plant the tallest plant first, in this instance the maidenhair fern, and then add the other plants around it.

4 When the final plant is in place, fill any gaps between them with soil mix and scatter a tablespoon of plant food granules on the surface.

5 Mulch between the plants with a layer of clay granules. These are more attractive than soil mix and help retain moisture. Water and place in a light position, but out of direct sunlight. The arrangement will benefit from a regular fine spray with water.

Copper-bottomed Begonia

The stunningly marked leaves of this begonia are shown to great advantage in this old copper pot. The pot was an inexpensive purchase from a flea market, and was cleaned before use.

MATERIALS
Copper pot, 20 cm (8 in) diameter
Lemon
Slow-release plant food granules
Clay granules

PLANTS
Begonia

begonia

1 Rub the tarnished pot with half a lemon. The acidity of the juice will quickly clean the pot, but don't overclean it or it will look brand new and lose some of its character.

2 Place the begonia, in its plastic pot, in the copper pot. Scatter a teaspoon of plant food granules on the surface of the soil mix.

GARDENER'S TIP
Other houseplants recommended for this type of treatment are the *Streptocarpus, Gynura* and cyclamen.

Plant at any time of the year.

3 Surround the plant with clay granules. Place in a light, but not sunny, position and water regularly.

Potted Palm

The classic "parlor" palm has been popular since Victorian times. It is a good-natured and attractive indoor plant and looks good in both traditional or contemporary settings.

MATERIALS AND TOOLS
Terracotta or plastic pot,
   30 cm (12 in) diameter
Styrofoam or similar draining material
Container soil mix
Slow-release plant food granules
Bark mulch

PLANTS
Kentia palm

Kentia *palm*

1 Half-fill the pot with broken styrofoam. It makes effective lightweight drainage material for the base of the pot.

2 Stand the palm in the pot and surround the rootball with container soil mix, pressing it firmly around the plant. Scatter a tablespoon of plant food granules on the surface.

3 Cover the soil mix with a layer of bark then water. Place in a position that receives good light, but no more than a couple of hours of direct sunlight each day. Water regularly during growing season, but allow the soil mix to dry out between waterings during the winter.

GARDENER'S TIP

Like most houseplants, the palm will benefit from being stood outside during warm summer rain. A good soaking shower removes dust from the leaves and gives the plant the benefit of a drink of untreated water.

Plant at any time of the year.

Colorful Kitchen Herbs

Make a bright and cheerful statement by using painted tins as containers for your kitchen herbs, often now available as plants from most supermarkets.

MATERIALS AND TOOLS
Empty food tins
White spirit
Masking tape
Paintbrush
Gloss paint

PLANTS
Dill
Chives
Parsley
Coriander
Basil

basil

parsley

coriander

1 Thoroughly wash and dry the tins. Use white spirit to remove any residual spots of glue. Wrap masking tape around the lip of the tins so that half of it protrudes above the rim.

2 Fold the masking tape inside the rim of the tins.

3 Paint the tins and leave them to dry.

4 Depending on the colors you choose some of them may need more than one coat.

5 When the tins are completely dry, simply remove the cellophane sleeve from each plant and place them, pot and all, into separate tins. Stand in a light position and water if the soil mix dries out.

GARDENER'S TIP

Large painted tins make colorful planters in the garden. Ask your local restaurant or school for some of the catering-size tins that they normally throw away.

Plant at any time of the year.

Counter-top Cactus Garden

Planting a bowl of cacti may take a little care and patience, but once achieved they will reward you by asking nothing more than benevolent neglect.

MATERIALS AND TOOLS
Terracotta bowl, 25 cm (10 in) diameter
Cactus soil mix
Old newspaper
Cactus gravel
Trowel or scoop

PLANTS
Euphorbia submammilaris
Rebutia muscula
Rose pincushion (*Mammilaria zeilmanniana*)
Cheiridopsis candidissima
Astrophytum ornatum
Prickly pear (*Opuntia*)

prickly pear

Rebutia muscula

rose pincushion

Astrophytum ornatum

1 Fill the bowl with cactus soil mix to within 5 cm (2 in) of the rim.

2 Prepare a thickly folded strip of newspaper to help you handle the cacti.

3 Plan your arrangement of the plants by standing them, in their pots, in the terracotta bowl.

4 Scoop a hollow in the soil mix for each plant as you work. Ease less prickly plants from their pots, surround them with a newspaper collar and lift into place.

5 Handle more ferocious plants carefully. Place the newspaper collar firmly around the plant while you ease it out of its pot. Carefully lower it into position. Leave the really prickly cacti until last or you will stab yourself on them as you are planting the other cacti.

6 Use a trowel to fill in around the plants with extra soil mix if needed. Add a finishing touch with a top-dressing of fine cactus gravel. Stand in good light and water sparingly.

GARDENER'S TIP

If cacti are just too aggressive for you, plant a succulent garden instead; they require the same treatment, but are free of thorns. If there are young children in your household be sure to choose the site of your cactus garden with care.

Plant at any time of the year.

Combined Effects

Displaying houseplants in groups creates a humid microclimate, which the plants prefer to the dry atmosphere of most homes. The humidity is increased by standing the pots in saucers of wet gravel kept moist by regular watering. Choose plants of contrasting shapes and sizes for the most striking effect.

GARDENER'S TIP

Bear in mind the background for your display when choosing your plants. Large architectural leaves and strong plain colors won't get lost against a "busy" wallpaper, whereas lots of variegations and color are better against a plain background.

Plant at any time of the year.

MATERIALS AND TOOLS
4 pots of various sizes with saucers
Crocks
Houseplant soil mix
Gravel

PLANTS
Lily
Maidenhair fern (*Adiantum*)
Cretan fern
Variegated creeping fig (*Ficus pumila*)

lily

Cretan fern

creeping fig

maidenhair fern

1 Place the crocks in the bottom of the pots.

2 Be sure the proportion of pot and plant is correct; these lilies are approximately the same height as the pot. Remove the lilies from their plastic pots and position in the pot.

3 Fill gaps around the rootballs with soil mix, pressing down firmly to avoid any air spaces.

4 Remove the foliage plants from their plastic pots and plant in the other containers, again filling in with soil mix where necessary. Water the plants thoroughly.

5 Fill the saucers with gravel. Stand the pots in their saucers and position the plants in good light, but away from direct sun. Keep the gravel in saucers damp and water the plants when soil mix dries out.

Water-loving Plants

The sweet flag is a marsh plant which loves the moist conditions in most bathrooms. Planted in gravel in a stylish glass pot or vase, it is easy to see when the water needs freshening.

MATERIALS AND TOOLS
Glass vase or pot, 20 cm (8 in) diameter
Gravel
Scoop

PLANTS
1 large or 2 small sweet flags (*Acorus gramineus* 'variegatus')

sweet flag

GARDENER'S TIP

The umbrella plant (*Cyperus alternifolius*) will also thrive in these conditions.

Plant at any time of the year.

1 Fill the bottom half of the container with gravel.

2 Take the plants out of their existing pots and place them on the gravel.

3 Fill the pot with gravel to the base of the leaves and half-fill the container with water. Place on a light windowsill and never allow the plants to dry out.

Dramatic Datura

The *Datura* or angel's trumpet, a popular conservatory plant, will grow enormous in time, providing it is planted in a large container and given regular food and water. The plant will benefit from a period outdoors during the summer, but will grow happily indoors the rest of the year.

MATERIALS AND TOOLS
Deep planter, at least 40 cm (16 in) diameter
Styrofoam or similar drainage material
Gloves
Equal mix loam-based soil mix and container soil mix
Slow-release plant food granules

PLANTS
Angel's trumpet (*Datura suaveolens*)
4 white busy lizzie (*Impatiens*)

1 Fill the base of the container with lightweight styrofoam or drainage material.

2 Use gloves to handle the angel's trumpet. Lift it into the container and pour soil mix around the edges of the plant, pressing down firmly around the rootball. Scatter 2 tablespoons of slow-release plant food granules on the surface of the soil mix.

angel's trumpet

busy lizzie

3 Plant the buzy lizzie around the base of the angel's trumpet, and remember to water frequently. Like most conservatory plants, the angel's trumpet will benefit from being stood outdoors in the summer. This is additionally recommended as the scent of the flowers can have a narcotic effect in confined spaces.

GARDENER'S TIP

All parts of the angel's trumpet are poisonous, and it should be handled with care. It is not recommended in households with small children. While it is sensible to be cautious, it is also a fact that many commonly cultivated plants are poisonous. For example, with the exception of its tubers, the potato plant is poisonous, as are *Dieffenbachia* and *Oleander*.

Plant in spring.

ACKNOWLEDGEMENTS

The authors and publishers would like to thank the following for their invaluable help:

Chelsea Gardener, 125 Sydney Street, London SW3, for providing containers.

Country World, Crews Hill, Enfield, for providing locations for step photography.

Brenda Hyatt, 1 Toddington Crescent, Blue Bell Hill, Chatham, Kent, for providing the auriculas on page 28.

Peter McHoy for the photographs on pages 12 and 13 left.

Tree Heritage, North Road, Hertford, for providing the Japanese maple on page 25.